better together*

*This book is best read together, grownup and kid.

 akidsco.com

a
kids
book
about

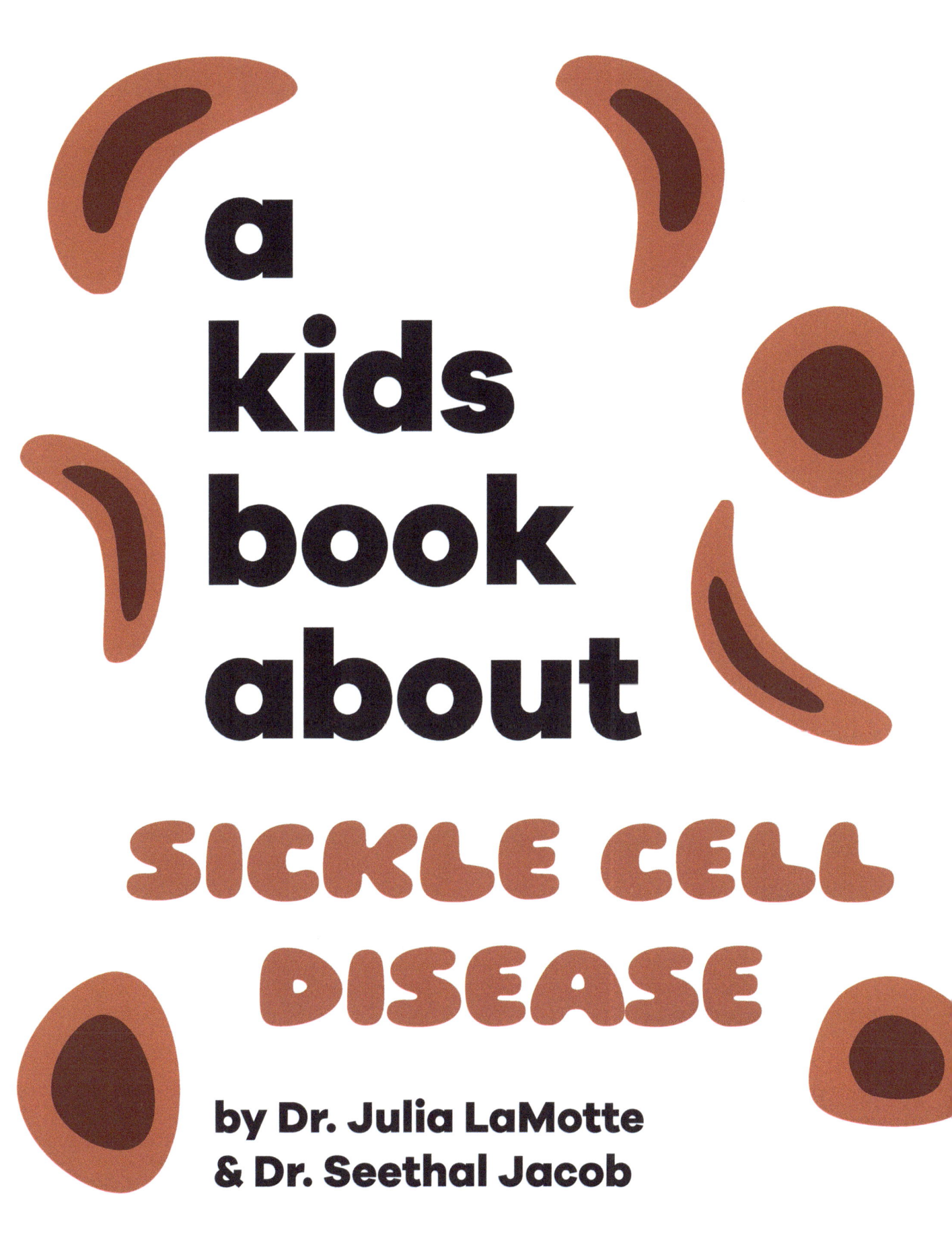

a kids book about

Text and design copyright © 2024
by A Kids Book About, Inc.

Copyright is good! It ensures that work like this can exist, and more work in the future can be created.

All rights reserved. No part of this publication may be reproduced, distributed, or transmitted in any form or by any means, including photocopying, recording, other electronic or mechanical methods, without the prior written permission of the publisher, except in the case of brief quotations embodied in critical reviews and certain other noncommercial uses permitted by copyright law. For permission requests, write to the publisher.

A Kids Book About, Kids Are Ready, and the colophon 'a' are trademarks of A Kids Book About, Inc.

Printed in the United States of America.

A Kids Book About books are available online: *akidsco.com*

To share your stories, ask questions, or inquire about bulk purchases (schools, libraries, and nonprofits), please use the following email address: *hello@akidsco.com*

Print ISBN: 979-8-89281-064-7
Ebook ISBN: 979-8-89281-065-4

Designed by Jelani Memory
Edited by Emma Wolf

Thank you to our family and friends for supporting us and all of our wild ideas.

Thank you to our sickle cell team members, whose generosity and dedication have built a program grounded in acceptance and trust.

Thank you to the sickle cell community and our patients. Your spirit and strength are inspiring, and we are so grateful to be entrusted with your care.

Intro

Whether you are a caregiver, a child with this disease, a sibling, a friend, a school teacher, or a community member, we hope this book brings light to what sickle cell disease is.

Every person living with sickle cell has a unique story to tell. This book reflects the numerous people we've encountered who live with or love someone with sickle cell, and may not fully reflect everyone's lived experience.

It is meant to help kids understand what sickle cell disease really is, how it has been overlooked, and how they can help support and advocate for kids living with sickle cell.

Let's dive into this topic, together.

Have you heard of **Sickle Cell Disease** before?

A lot of people think it's a disease having to do with blood.

And that's not exactly wrong...
but it's not the whole truth either.

That's why we wrote this book!

Do you know what our blood is made of?

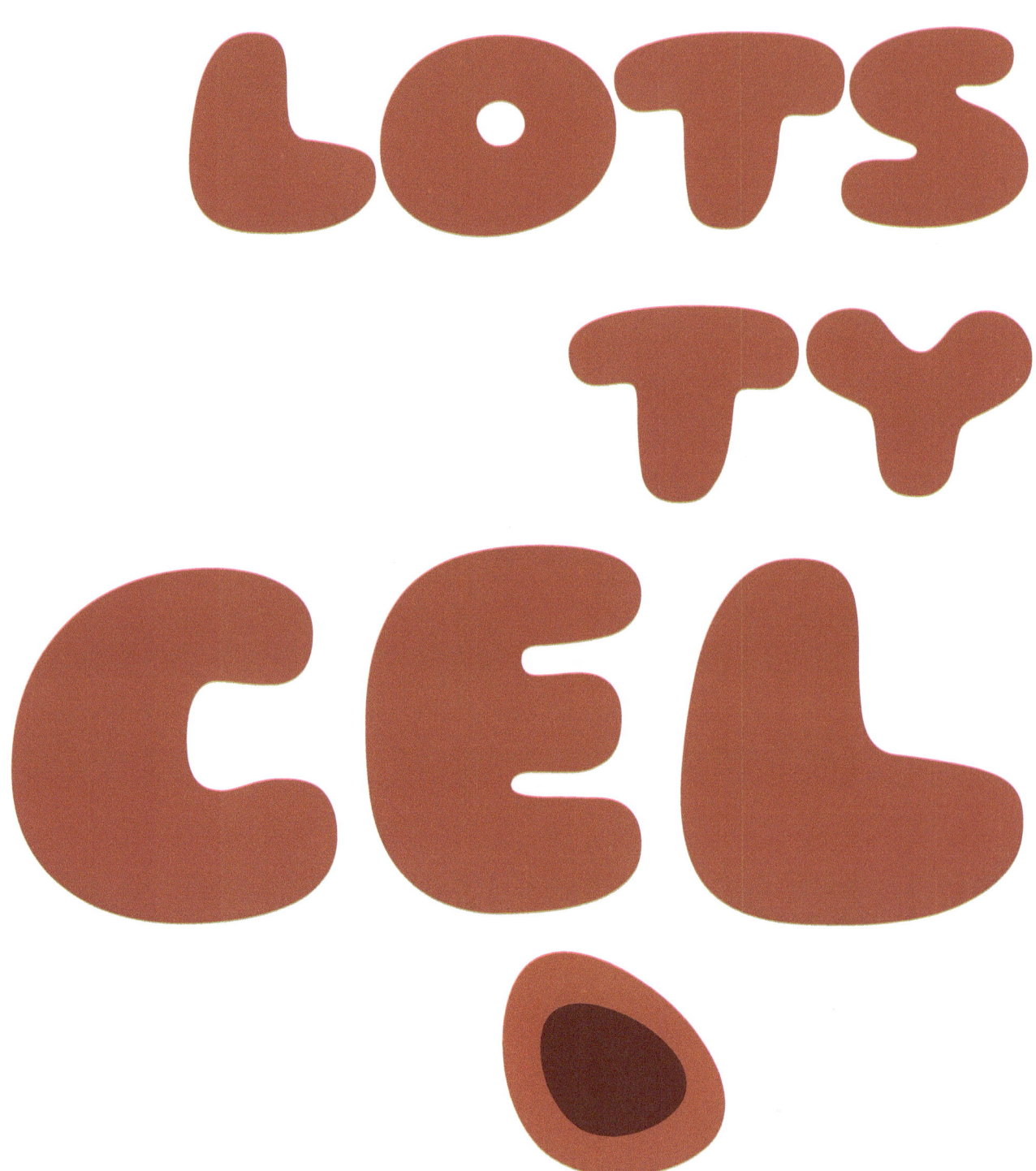

They're all important and help us breathe, move, play...do everything!

One of the most important types is the

Red blood cells give our blood the color it is (get it? **R E D** blood cells!), but they also carry oxygen throughout our whole bodies, from our head to our toes.

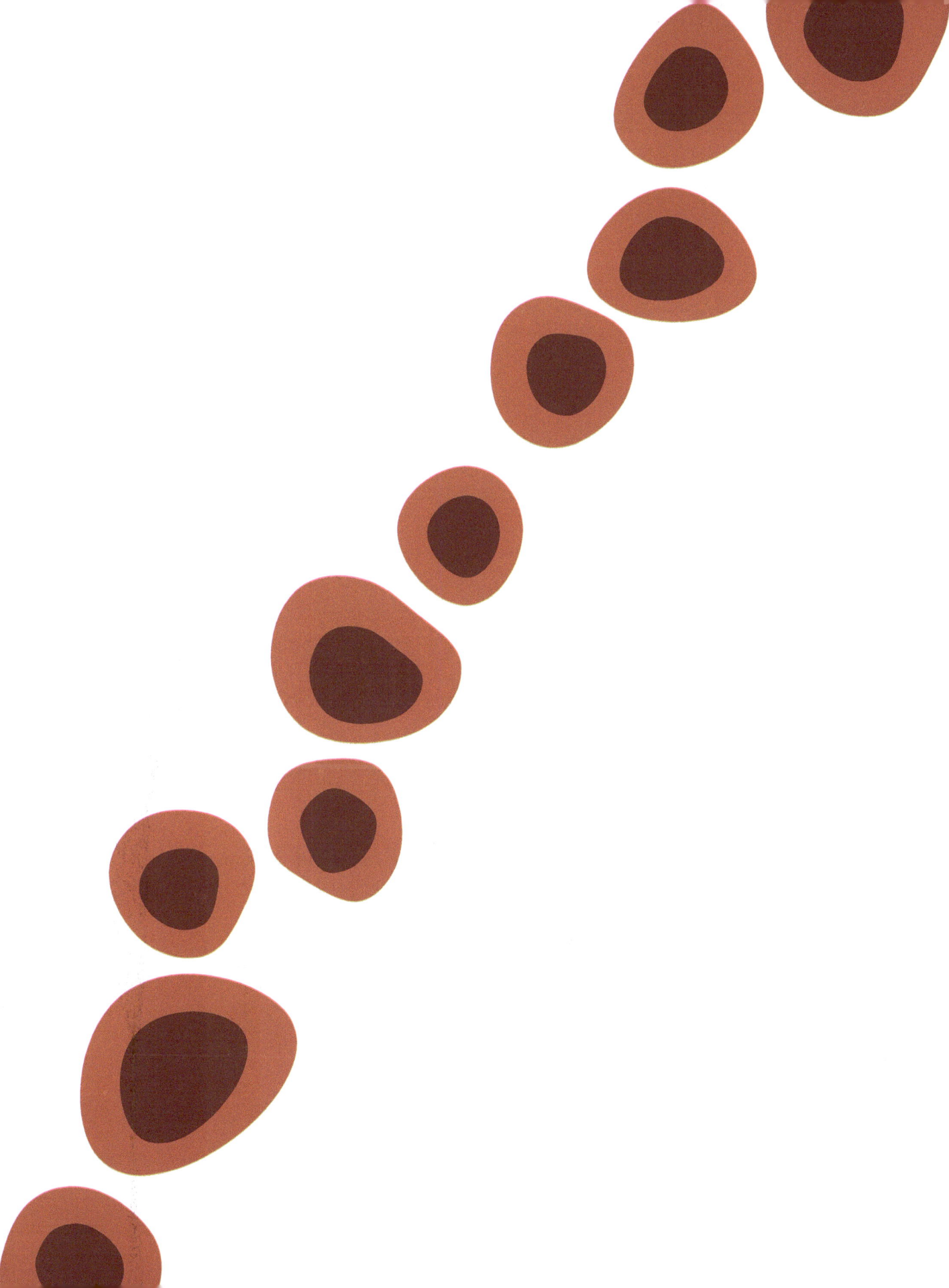

Inside each red blood cell are tiny clusters of protein called **hemoglobin**.

Hemoglobin holds onto the oxygen for transportation and lets it go when it gets to a part of the body which needs it.

With sickle cell disease, there's 1 tiny mutation, or change, in 1 gene that causes someone's hemoglobin to look different.

Red blood cells are generally shaped like a squishy donut (without the hole!).

They are flexible and move through small parts of the body easily.

When your hemoglobin lets go of the oxygen, it changes shape and causes the red blood cell to sickle.

(Get it? Sickle + cell.)

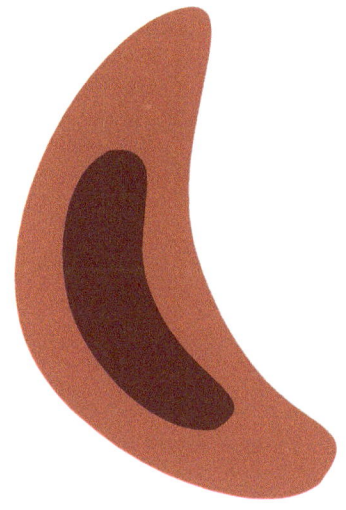

This sickle shape can look like a banana or a half moon, with pointed ends.

Sometimes, when those sickled red blood cells move through narrow parts of the body, they can get caught.

Sickled red blood cells will pile on top of each other and can block blood flow to important parts of the body like your brain, lungs, kidneys...everywhere!

This can lead to severe pain, cause anemia*, and many other complications that aren't always visible.

*Anemia is when your body doesn't have enough red blood cells.

(This is why it's important to stay connected with your sickle cell care team!)

So, sickle cell disease
is definitely about the blood.

But it's about WAY more than that.

It's important to know that each person with sickle cell experiences it

ently.

Maybe you're wondering,

Do I have sickle cell?

Sickle cell is something you're born with, which means you inherited it from your biological parents.

(It is not contagious!)

It takes 2 mutations to make sickle cell disease: 1 from each biological parent.

Some people have 1 mutation, and this means they have sickle cell trait.*

*People with the trait can pass the disease along to their biological children.

This mutation was first discovered in parts of the world where many people have malaria*, because the pointed cells actually helped to protect AGAINST malaria infections.

*Malaria is a disease that infects red blood cells and is transmitted to people by mosquitoes.

This includes places like Africa and India.

So, sickle cell is most common in that part of the world, as well as the Caribbean and Latin America.

Here, in the United States, a majority of people with sickle cell are Black or African American.

Even though it's the MOST common inherited blood disease in the WORLD, we still don't know nearly enough about it.

For example, there are only 4 medicines available to treat sickle cell—3 of which were approved in the last 5 years!

And we've known about the disease since the 1800s!

The answers are both complicated and pretty simple.

Money is needed to fund research, and research can lead to new treatments.

But sickle cell doesn't receive nearly enough money for research.

This is because the people most affected are those whose voices haven't been listened to throughout history.

Other inherited diseases whose affected populations look different receive way more funding and attention, even though they affect less people.

That doesn't sound very fair, does it?

We aren't saying that 1 disease is more important than another.

We believe everyone deserves the resources they need to thrive.

And I bet you do, too!

So, what do we do now?

First, we need to listen.

Everyone's pain is different, and it's not always obvious.

It matters that we believe and validate what they say.

A lot of times, when people with sickle cell describe their pain, it isn't taken seriously.

An X-ray machine helps us see broken bones, but we don't have a machine to help us make sense of others' pain.

And, it goes beyond pain.

Sometimes, symptoms can look like changes in focus in school, having trouble finishing homework, or feeling tired.

Symptoms of sickle cell can be physical, mental, and emotional, and all of them matter.

It's like we said—

IT'S WAY MORE THAN JUST BLOOD.

And now you know that, because you're reading this book!

Information is powerful!
And there's a lot of misinformation about this disease.

You can work against that and spread power through your words.

And, our actions matter, too.

Many kids with sickle cell feel different from their peers.

But they shouldn't have to.

kind
& emp
o go
long

ness
athy
a
way!

If there's someone in your life with sickle cell, you might want to ask how you can support them.

Even though we still have a lot to learn, we can all work together toward a more understanding future.

And if you're a kid with sickle cell, we want to say thank you.

Kids like you have inspired our work and fuel what we do every day to improve the lives of people with this disease.

You are more than
how others define you.

You get to choose how BIG or
little sickle cell is in your life.

The possibilities are endless!

Outro

To all those living with sickle cell disease, and their families: we see you. We want you to know we appreciate you and hope our work can improve even the smallest piece of what you experience. We also want you to know there are so many advocates like us out there.

To those who know a child living with sickle cell disease, we hope this book helps you begin to understand what they are experiencing. But we also hope you don't stop here!

If you want to learn more about sickle cell disease, take a look at these resources:

www.sicklecelldisease.org

www.cdc.gov/ncbddd/sicklecell/index.html

If you are an educator working with a child who has sickle cell disease, you may notice changes before anyone else. You are a really important part of their care team! Check out these resources for more information on how you can help:

www.scdcoalition.org/uploads/SCDC-Build-Your-Own-SCD-School-Binder_print.pd

About The Authors

Dr. Julia LaMotte (she/her) spent her childhood exploring libraries and bookstores throughout New England where her parents instilled a lifelong love of reading. She is a pediatric psychologist who supports kids with medical conditions. She is also an active educator to future physicians and psychologists and believes change is possible only through knowledge.

Dr. Seethal Jacob (she/her) is a physician who leads a pediatric sickle cell program, and her life's work focuses on improving the care people with sickle cell disease are provided. She loves doing this by seeing kids in her clinic, and by understanding the ways in which families access medical care as a health services researcher.

Together, they have been able to advocate on behalf of this community and their work has been recognized both locally and nationally for their creative approaches.

 @julia-lamotte-phd   @seethal-j

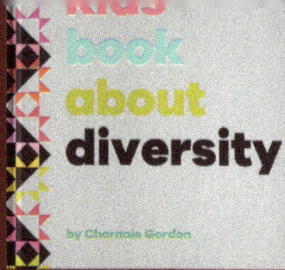

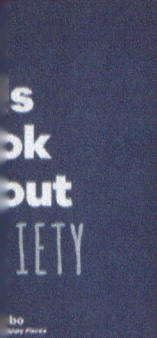

Discover more at akidsco.com

www.ingramcontent.com/pod-product-compliance
Lightning Source LLC
Chambersburg PA
CBHW061359010526
44107CB00012B/992